Copyright © 2006 Audrey D Simmons

No part of this publication
May be reproduced in any form, except
for the purposes of review, without
prior written permission from
the copyright owner.

The right of Audrey Simmons to be identified as author
of this work has been asserted by her in accordance with
the Copyright, Designs and Patents Act, 1988

All rights reserved.

Published by
ads
PO Box 50056

Dedicated to my mother and father, my family, and friends, to my sisters at CWWAs all of whom have help me put this book together. Without their love and support this project may never have got off the ground.

Unofficial Birthday

I looked over my shoulder
And saw the sun rise,
My loc's swinging down my back,
Sankofa on my right side,
Ankh on my left,
My vision is becoming clearer
My strength renewed,
I think I'll call it morning,
My new world
My new day
My new self,
I think I'll call it morning

Contents

Chapter 1 First Steps
Welcome to my country	7
We west Indians	8
The journey to myself	10
African Dementia	11
I need to start acting big	13
The union Jack ain't my home	16
The vagrant	18
Mumma can sing	19
Reflection	21
Dry han' man	23
Yuh grandmother's voice	26
Lost love	28
Why do I read Shakespeare?	30
Ancestry	31
Bastard name	34

Chapter 2 Women steps
I am woman	37
The plea of a desperate	41
If history were a women	44
The 400 year journey to me	45
Reappearance	50
I wish….(one of my bad days)	51
A Black woman step by step guide to giving her man fulfilment in the bedroom	53
No way natural	57

Contents...

Chapter 3 Baby steps
Black acorn	61
A call to arms	62
Moonlight	66
Identity crisis	67
Little twang	69
Childhood	71

Chapter 4 Man steps
Umbrella love	74
The key to a man's heart	76
A warning to the black man	78
Tears	80
Black sunshine	81
Clearing out my heart	83
Deaf Girls	84

Welcome to my country

Welcome to my country,
Sorry did I say my country,
I meant my country,
A country that my taxes own.

Come to my country,
I do mean my country,
Is this my country
Because I have no where else to go?

You're in my country,
At least I think it's my country,
I have a country,
My fore–fathers fought
To make it so.

Welcome to my country,
Yes I said my country,
Born here, grew here, am here,
This is my country,
Although others say go.

This is my country,
Truly my country,
Brought in from other countries
To help your country grow,

This is not my country,
It's never been my country,
Born here, grew here, not really here,
Welcome to my country
         My country
                 My country

We West Indians

I am who you used to be,
You were an Arawark, a Carib,
The first natives of the West Indies.
You are still you
And I am still me,
But is there a thread of you
Running through the coconut tree
Does the earth still carry your spirit,
And has it mingled with the sugar cane juice
And that's why it tastes so sweet,
Is there some remnant of you,
That tells me whose space I now occupy
Does the sound of the hurricane that whistles across the island,
Carry your distance and now forgotten cry.

I know if I cock my ears and listen,
I can hear
Your moccasin covered footsteps
running and dancing 'round fireside
As if you were still here.
Your shadow moving past
with elegance and dignity,
Is that your chanting voice singing in the early morning breeze,
And does the hummingbird that flies so high,
Have your eyes and that you are watching over we; the caretakers of your legacy.

We are inextricably bound
by our different histories,
You are still you
And I am still me
But I am now who you used to be,
The native of the West Indies

The journey to my self

The journey to myself,
Starts with a robbery,
The crime of centuries
Over looked, passed by
As if I'm a living lie,
The transportation,
Exploitations,
Work without liberation,
They think I died,
But there are a billion voices in my heart
That keep pushing me forward,
A single voice in my soul
That makes me step forward,
Onward with the journey to myself.

African Dementia

Old woman sitting in the corner,
Who you be?
Your face looks familiar
And you almost look like me,

You red skin, dark skin woman,
With the curly straight hair,
Wearing a kentè sari
And a diamond broach in your hair,

You barefoot woman
With the slippers spun from gold,
Sitting silently in the corner
Telling stories yet to be told,

Let me come a little closer, so I can see,
Your green, blue, brown eyes
That are laughing with pain
And smiling sadly at me,

I know you old woman
But I can't place you all the same,
You're the person no ones ever heard of,
With the famous name,

Stand up old woman,
Before up tumble down,
And them lock you up
In an open prison
To give you your freedom,

Close your eyes old woman
So that you can see,
Your past life before you,
You can become who you used to be,

Wrap up old somebody,
You don't see how the day is hot,
Dementia has made your mind clearer
And you have remembered the
things you forgot,

You are many old woman
With a single name,
Ethiopia, Ghana, Africa, home
You are all one and the same

I need to start acting big

I need to start acting big,
Time to tek the responsibility,
Mumma and papa time over
Now is me.

Mumma, put up yuh tired foot,
Rest back yuh weary head,
Old time struggling over,
Time for you to be led,

Papa, put down de staff
That carry yuh, over ocean wide
Close up yuh eye,
Let all thoughts slide
To less stressful ting instead,

Look back over yuh shoulder,
See how far yuh come,
From when Teddy boys used to try to
Pick you off one by one.
Yuh 'member dem time day papa
Yuh 'member dem time day mom
When counting out yuh money took longer,
'cas it was in pence, shilling and pounds

Britain gave out a great cry to the colonies,
To come over to de mother lan'
'cas it was down on it's knee

When Windrush lan' a Tilbury dock
Dem never know what lick dem,
Dem never t'ought dey would live fe see
Black man a broke bread with dem,

Nurses, postmen, electrician,
Yuh did come, one and all,
Start to build likkle foundation,
Start chipping at de colonial wall,
But dat must have been back breaking wok
And I can see in yuh eyes,
That yuh is dog tired
Of fighting for dat prize

So mumma, don't tink I'm not grateful
Papa don't tink I don't care,
But now is time to hand over de baton
And step-a-side,
I tink is only fair,
that me the younger one
Carry on, making our voices heard,
Using the knowledge that you gave me,
Passing on what I've learnt

So mumma put up yuh tired foot,
Papa rest back yuh weary head
Old time struggling over
Time for you to be led

I need to start acting big
Time to tek the responsibility
Mumma and papa time over,
Now it's up to you and me

The Union Jack ain't my home

De Union Jack in a mi back
A draw me dung to de grung.
Dem say dat de red, white and blue is not fe me,
Is just a club wey dem use fe abuse
We de Black born of dis lan'.

De Union Jack was me swaddling clothes
Mamma wrap im up and tell me fe gwan,
Be better than she, be strong, be free,
Dat dis is de lan' of OPPO-TUNE-NITY

Me a look in her face
De face dat dis lan' dun with
De push me pull me face dat
Mark-up like a chile first picture

Me look 'pon her hand
De han' dat cold weather gnarl-up
De carry go bring come han' dat raise me

Me look 'pon de body
De body dat full of yum, banana and breshea,
De body dat give up life fi me,
To be free, here in dis lan' of OPPO-TUNE-NITY

She still have me swaddling clothes
De one dat she wrap me in to be better than she
To be strong, to be free
But de colour fade—wash out

But cas of de yam, banana and breshea dat feed me
De push me pull me face dat look me
De carry go bring come han' dat raise me,
I can say CAT-TA-GOR-ICALLY
Dat me is free from de swaddling clothes an
De Union Jack dat in a me back a draw me dung to de
grung

The Vagrant

I see a man
At least I think it's a man,
It's a shadow of a man,
An imprint of a man,
A stain of a man,
A fossilised impression of a man,
A life beaten outline of a man,
A clothed, empty shell of a man,
A walking carcass,
But a man none the less

Mumma Can sing

Mumma can sing
Voice like a mischievous angel,
High notes wrapped in linen
Trained she is not
But, up there on those high notes
Her voice trembles and rattles
Like it is bouncing of an unpadded cell,
It's all up there by it self,
Roaming, all straight laced and high neck blouse,
Spiritually guiding,
Telling you about God
Of his greatness, salvation.

Mumma's voice
Can smile at you,
Disapprove of you,
Chastise you and
Love you all at the same time,
Without missing a note,
Without skipping a beat,
In time, on time,
'lord lift me up and make a stand'

One eye on the song sheet
The other on the congregation
Don't do anything that you shouldn't
Or the voice will know and tell on you,

Mumma's voice is all seeing
All knowing
Omnipotent in its humbleness,
Afraid of no one, some voices are better than mumma's
Rounder, softer, smoother,
But I could never pick them out from the crowed
Who wants all that honey and no lime?

Other voices challenge hers,
Bully her, try to put her down,
But mumma's voice raises its self higher,
Grows wings and flies
The tremble and the rattle
Stand up like tail feathers,

That is mumma's voice,
In church on Sabbath
With a hat on,
Mumma dressed in black and white
Her voice high notes wrapped in linen
Like a mischievous angel,
Mumma can sign

Reflection

Who is this that stands before me
This gnarled up, chewed up
Somebody that stands in front of me,
Hair as white as bammy,
Teeth darken from the cold
Work days over, time to rest,
              And wait, and see.

Strong bone someone that you used to be
Is no more, you're gone

Back bone twist-up with unfulfilled expectancy,
Mouth motionless, all you wanted to say still not said,
Eyes as weak as the English tea,
They're tired, tired of seeing friends dying,
leaving you behind,
              To wait and see,

Knees bend, as once again it's raining,
The strong bone someone
that you used to be is no more,
              You're gone,

Who is dis dat dey before me?
Only memories of who you used to be,
To keep you warm, your one company,
The strong bone some that walked
The water to this land,
With clear mind and clear complexion
Now looks in the mirror and asks
Who is this that stands before me?

DRY HAN' MAN

Dry han' stretch out before me
Like a discoloured black lace table cloth,
Han' look like it's been washed in ashes,
Ain't seen Coco Butter since nineteen long time,
Olive oil a distant memory,
Astral's name forgotten,
Banished into history along with
Shower gel and Lynx after shave.

Dry han' begging likkle change,
A few pence to get him through his day,
What's your story dry han'?

Weren't you the dry han'
That travel to this lan' with hopes
As high as mountain tops
And dreams in abundance?
Alight from the boat in your Sunday best,
Yuh hat tilted slightly to the left
Smile as wide as gallies end,
Polished and shine,
Get likkle work, pay likkle bills
Throw you pardna first and last,
Buy you house 'pon top of de hill,
De only place them would let yuh have

De bottle mek yuh see everything clear,
It get to yuh dry han'?

Wat happen dry han'
Working the morning, noon and night shift
To provide likkle life style,
Money no nuff
Ends nar meet
Weekend time yuh only release,
Tenants, Brandy, Vodka—cheers,

Britain pressure tek yuh,
Baby shirt don't fit yuh,
But you had to squeeze init and galong,
And when hell pop and everything crash,
The system look and shook it's head and said
Schizophrenic, manic depressive a danger to the world
Lock him up
Tek yuh out of circulation,
Yuh tek yuh drugs 3 times a day,
Sat in de communal room
Watching you life style slip away,

Children don't utter yuh name,
Gran' pickney a grow and a do de same,
Yuh wife run of wid mister sof' han'
Cos dem don't know and can't understand'
Why Papa lost him mind,
De NHS a do it's best, but,
with cuts and nurses shortages
Yuh a get back less than them tek from yuh over de years,
What happen dry han'
De dream flop,
Come, see some change here, is all me have,
Tek it and buy some tea,
A mash mouth smile look up where false teet' should be,
Eyes moist, yellow like 2 day old turn cornmeal,
Jump with glee,
What really happen dry han'?
Why yuh a stand a street side
Asking me for a few penny to get yuh through yuh day.

YUH GRANDMOTHER VOICE

Don't forget to look up to the sky
The voice in my head said,
You need the stars to guide you
I nodded in agreement
Then saw something on the ground
Bent down to pick it up
It was shiny and round and new
Held my attention, held my head down

Don't forget to spread your wings
The voice in my head said
The wind will take you far in life
 I ignored it
 Preferring to tie them behind my back
So that they wouldn't get in the way
I run from place to place
A wild child, to busy learning new things
Such matters could wait.

Don't forget that many make one
I shrug my shoulders,
Not understanding the statement
Strength comes from within
I am strong, I will survive
I can't listen to such nonsense

Then I trip; fall awkwardly,
An untidy heap on the ground
I Can't get up
I've lost my way,

Don't forget…
I hear the voice in my head
Like it was there for the first time

I look up to the sky
To see where the voice is coming from
A trillion black faces
That resemble me
But are not me, look down, smiling,
In unison, they pick me up
I have the strength to carry on,

Don't forget to
Look up to the sky,
Spread your wings,
Out of many we are one,
Simple really

LOST LOVE

The ash white streaks down
the backs of her legs
Suggest that she had wet
herself recently,
A half chewed cigar hangs
from the corner of her mouth:unlit,

> *Someone somewhere is saying*
> *Mum's not well,*
> *Hasn't been for a long time,*
> *Really miss her at Christmas*

Her hair is a bad Afro
Dented on one side,
A mass of white bush,
Dotted with patches of black,
The second hand coat is wrapped
around a braless chest,
Tired feet are stuffed into
someone else's badly fitting shoes.

Someone, somewhere has a memory,
The face of a women
With a warm smile that they now cling to
for comfort,
Mum's not well, hasn't be well for ages,
I really miss her at Christmas,

Her eyes are busy, looking for something that can't be seen,
Her cigar goes round and round in her month,
In time with the bounce in her walk to no where,

Someone, somewhere shed's a silent tear
For the love they've lost,
England's pressure took her mind away
I really miss her at Christmas

WHY DO I READ SHAKESPEARE?

Why do I read Shakespeare?
Because I can

When Bill was putting quill to paper
I was being transported across the seas,

When the round house
Was at the height of its fame
I was at my lowest ebb
Stuck at the bottom of the master's shoe

I couldn't read it then
But I can now…… Smile!

ANCESTRY

I wish I did now my mudda's mudda,
Or her mudda, de one dem did call Grace
And I wonder if she is the one
dat give me dis big butty.

I wonder if great grand daddy Joe
was long and straight,
And dat's why me brother long
like post dem use fe hold up gate,

I wonder if great Auntie Ditty
Was de wayward one
Who give me my big feet,
Or if great great uncle Butty 'pon
my mudda's side
Give my cousin Michael 'im buck teet'

I wonder if I could look at some
old pictures of my ancestry,
If I would see my owner mout'
A look back and a laugh at me,
When I look in de mirror who's eyes
are reflecting back, Are they mine?
Or do they belong to
great great great uncle Cuthbert,
If I was to look hard, hard over my shoulder could I see,
My great great great grand mudda's ,fadda
Standing in a long line and a dance de quadrille and a
wave at me,
I wonder if me look in her face,
If me will see,
Someone with my mout' my nose, my eyes,
Someone who look just like me

I wonder if me work back through me genealogy
And pick pick through me DNA
Me can trace back mi family tree
Piece by piece put myself together
To 400 years ago,

To a young women from de Ashanti tribe
Sitting by a river,
A wash out two piece a clothes

I wonder if me look in her face,
If me will see,
Someone with my mout', my nose , my eyes,
Someone who look just looked me.

BASTARD NAME

Are you asking me my name?
You want my surname,
My second name,
My family name,
You think I should know

                                        Don't you?

You think, seeing as my parents
Are married,
My name will give me my heritage?
That it denotes my lineage,
That if I step backwards,
Step upwards, step round-wards,
I will find myself

                                        Don't you?

My name, shouts out to me,
Tells me, I'm a bastard child,
My name was born out of wed-lock
My name proves your rape of me

                                        Doesn't it?

You thought that if I signed my name
A thousand times,
If I saw it in lights,
Neon signs, T.V credits
I would accept it,
Let it represent me

                                         Didn't you

Signed on the dotted line
My name, my surname, my family name,
Makes me mis-present myself,
Lets you hide openly your past,
Lets you feel comfortable around me,

                                         Don't you?

My name, is your name,
Your alphabetical shame,
Given by force,
Taken with reluctance
I hold it up as banner
To show you up

                                         Are you?

My name reflects that
I am a bastard child,
Your bastard child,
My name tells me so

Chapter 2
Women steps

I am woman

I am woman,
Conceived on a bed of false truths,
half-truths and lies,
Forced form my mother into a world
where my destiny is pre-designed,

My navel string is cut
and given to my mother to hold,
I am to take up the mantle that is my birth right,
My crown has been woven for me,
Using the thorns from their time and your time,
Each time she is punched, kicked
and beaten into submission,
Each time she caught him in a lie with
another women or other man,
Each time she is deserted to
raise her family alone,
My crown grew.

I am woman,
My breasts are more than mummeries,
They are my centrepiece,
Every man, woman and child has suckled,
So that they might grow-up, grow wise and leave,

They have nourished themselves
without thanks or appreciation,
But still the milk flows

Giving them time to rest,
While I worked,
Mashing corn, grinding flour

We are women,
Plant your navel string at the road side,
Watch it grow into a cool shady tree,
It will grow despite your pain,
Each time she is raped to satisfy his inadequacies,
Each time she ''dash wey her belly',
Because he's not ready for the responsibility,
Each time she sells her dignity on the street,
So he doesn't feel alone,
The tree will grow,
It will bare fruit so sweet,
But, you the owner cannot eat them,
They are for the next generation to feast on,
Before the mantle,
Before the crown,
Eat sweet fruit,
Navel string fruit,
This is my legacy

I am woman
Conceived on a bed of
False truths, half truths and lies,
Strong back, big breast, milk still flowing,
Mashing corn ,grinding flour,
Navel string tree still growing,
Eat fruit, sweet fruit,
My legacy.
I am woman

The Plea of a Desperate Woman

You want to go to Ann Summers with me to buy a sex toy?
A vibrating, pulsating piece of plastic
That have batteries supplied,
They have all different kinds of things
To suit your mood,
Oils, lotions, potions some you can even eat as food

Just come and have a look with me
Nobody nar see,
Me want look 'pon the vibrators
You can look 'pon the magazines,

Dey have sexy underwear yuh no
Yuh no want to see me in one thing?
How you mean be butty too big?
Ay watch yuh mout' boy, me no like how yuh a gwan,
Let's go up to the city
They have a great big shop
Lets buy an electronic, robotic plug in at the mains
Something us help F.... Make love

I want to be like Neil Armstrong
Garn to de moon,
I want you to dip into me repeatedly
With you big long spoon,

I want Mr long and strong
To take me on a ride of discovery,
I want you to find my A, B, G spot
With some whipped cream and a bowl of strawberries,

Just imagine the fun we could have
With handcuffs and the like
And you could ride me like a Honda civic
Or one of those Harley Davidson bikes,

I want to sing like de Temptations
In perfect harmony
I want you to ride me so hard
De light bulb just bun yuh batty

Just tek me to de Ann Summers shop
I begging you please,
You can buy anything you want
Just as long as it has a lead.

I want to plug and go
To de land of oh....
Sorry, what did you say, mi must
Pass yuh de remote control

If history were a women

If history were a women,
What colour would she be?
White like Madonna's virgin,
Or Black like Whoopi and me?

If history were a women,
How would she style her hair?
Would she pull it back into a spinster's bun,
Or have a duparta or head wrap there?

If history were a women
Whose make-up would she wear?
Maxfactor, Revlon, Rimmel,
Or Mary Kay and Fashion Fair?

If history were a women,
What language would she speak?
Would she have the dulcet tones
Of Romeo and Juliet,
Or the urban chat off the streets?

If history were a women
By what name would she be known?
Would she be Rebecca, Jane, Eugenie,
Or Nikisha, Melisha, Ngun?

If history were a women
How much different would it be?
Would it still be one dimensional lies
Masquerading as facts,
Or would it include the truth of everybody

The 400 year journey to me

I am me,
An old me,
A new me,
The 50 million, 100 million,
Million upon million of lost me's

I am the short me, the tall me,
The fast and wise me,
The me they threw off the
Tall ship, the long ship, the cargo ship.

I am the strength of the millions of me's
That went before,
I am their weakness, their canniness
I am their feistiness, their fearlessness
I am dispossessed.

I am their tongue-less whisper
Their voiceless scream,
Their agonising thought
Manifested into a walking dream

I am the armless shove
They could not give the master,

I am their sugar soaked soul,
Their molasses drenched hand
I am the throat that tastes the
Fruits of their labour,
Washed down with white rum
Dark rum and Black blood

I am the thousandth step to freedom
They never took,
The struggle they never lived
To see to the end,

I am the sun rise on a simple grave
Made of nothing more than a memory
Of whom they once were,
In a place far from home,
Now buried, namelessly,
In a place they had to call home.

I am the smile they held in their hearts,
The breath they never got to exhale,

I am their vision,
A wonder not seen, a thought,
A notion, an ancient tradition
That has become a tomorrow world.

I am a chant from motionless lips
That spoke a thousand words,
Words that fell to the ground,
Mingled with the cane juice
That the hummingbird now drinks.

I am a song,
A rhythm that flows in time with the rain
That washes away their pain
Into gleaming white sandy beaches.

I am ackee and cassava
Walked on brutality, hatred, lies
Walked on joy, triumph glory
To become chips and curry Pattie.

I am the drum, the bass,
The trumpet, the piano,

I am Salsa, Tango, Rumba, Marenge,
I am reggae, dancehall, hip-hop,
Jazz, rock and roll,

Without me your hips would not swing

I am Elvis, Emimem, Miles Davis,
Bob Marley , James Brown, Dizzy Rascal,

I am Ella Fitzgerald, Joss Stone,
Britney Spears, Beverly Knight,

Without me they would have no words to sing,

I am Mohammed Ali, Jessie Owens,
Ian Wright, Frank Bruno, Arthur Ash,

I am Nanny, Paul Bogle, Malcolm X,
Martin Luther King, Nelson Mandela,

I am blood, sweat, tears, lost fortune, stolen land.

I am weakness, bravado, lost identity,

I am happiness, opportunity, success,
Wrapped in a cloth of love, forgiveness, strength.

I am still here,
In spite of,
Despite all of this,

I am a glorious Diaspora,
I am a mouth piece to a silent voice that
Has never stopped shouting.

Reappearance

I looked in the books,
I didn't see myself.
I looked on the television,
I saw distorted versions of myself.
I listened to the radio,
The voice was quiet—unlike myself.
I read the newspaper,
I was presented with a different self.
I read the magazines,
I didn't look like myself.
I looked in the mirror.
And I couldn't see myself.

So

I listened to my mother's voice,
Who told me about myself,
I switched off the television,
So I could visualise myself,
I burnt the magazines,
So I could like myself,
I looked behind me,
To find myself

And I re-discovered me

I wish… (one of my bad days)

I wish I didn't feel so empty,
Wish I didn't feel so hollow
Wish I didn't feel like a huge
Oesophagus with nothing to swallow,

I wish I didn't feel like a cup
That's neither half empty or half full,
A pint of draught bitter
That nobody wants to pull

I wish I wasn't so boring
So tediously slow,
Lacking imagination,
Original thought,
I wish I still had my afro

I wish I didn't feel like
I live my life in a vacuum,
Swan around like atmospheric pus
Or a bowl of ice cream that neither
Child or adult want to consume

I wish I was somebody,
Anybody, but me,
Wish I could pluck my eyes out
Stick them in my gut, .
Looking outwards
So my emptiness can't be seen

I wish I didn't have this space
In the centre of myself
Someone, somewhere
Has the better half of me
Sitting on their shelf
And here I sit, the lesser me
Looking into my darkness
Just wishing my life away
A walking, breathing, living
CARCASS

A Black women's step by step guide to giving her man fulfilment in the bedroom

Step 1
To start your romantic interlude, a lubricant can be used. Smothered over the body to create that most sensual of feelings.

This could consist of body oil, olive oil or indeed any oil, but please be careful when using cooking oil as this has a tendency to ignite under fractious conditions.

For a man who may not have been introduced to such novel ways in the bedroom, a medium size tub of Astral moisturiser can be substituted. For the ruff necks amongst us, there is always Vaseline Petroleum Jelly, please make sure it's a large tub. This may not be as smooth going on, but there is the added benefit of being able to stick the ashtray to his chest, for his after the moment cigarette, safe in the knowledge that it will not slide off.

Step 2
To continue your sexual escapade, you can now introduce a little 'je ne sais quoi' into the proceedings, in the form of ice-cream, yoghurt, or for those of you whose palates are not used to such decadence, there is always a tin of Shake 'n' Squirt. Fruit can be added for decoration, depending on the time of year. Now for some black men the very idea of eating yoghurt is quite abhorrent to them, going against all their manly values, never mind ladies, this problem is easily remedied, simply replace the offending item with a tin of bully beef; onions optional, or for those men who have a little more sophistication, there is always a tin of Condensed milk, for the best results please use Nestlé.

Step 3

For those of you who are lucky enough to have roused your partner into actually performing the act of making love, and haven't been reduced to waiting for a quick-squeeze-on-the-left-breast-during-the-talkie-bits-of-match-of-the-day, congratulations, but this is not a time to rest on one's laurels, no, no ladies, we have to be sure that our man is enjoying this most intimate and precious moments. So ladies if your man is clinging to the headboard shouting 'I am Moses, I have stretch forth my rod of iron, parted the Black Seas and all is well', then you know that your work is done.

Step 4

Once this 15 minutes of togetherness is complete, and you are both basking under the light from your Ikea lamp, your mans should turn to you and lovingly say
'So warhappen, what yuh saying, it did alright?'
To which ladies you should reply
'Oh-yeah-yeah-baby, dat was wicked man'
Then he will continue with 'so yuh nar get mi a beer, an' you might as well get yourself one Babycham. Confirming just how much he cares.
Once the alcoholic beverage has been consumed, he will roll over, break wind loudly and fall into that instant deep sleep, that neither hurricane nor exploding bomb could ruse him from. Ladies it is at this point that you, with lighting speed and great dexterity, whip out your vibrator— mine is call goldie, but you can get them in a variety of colours—and **finish the Job**

No way natural

Yuh wan' loc's yuh hair?
Tun Bongo nutty Dred,
Go back to nappy curl
And' have dem worm
Like sing-ting in a yuh head.

Yuh turn all funky, funky,
Afro-centric tun yuh mad,
Like dem put yuh brains 'pon a plane
'back to Africa'
An' yuh good sense in a Kenté bag.

Yuh nuh see how de young girls dem dress,
Dark 'n' Loverly set di tren'
And if it wasn't for YAKI hair
I'm sure mi life would a en'

And as for de weave on,
De glue on and de pin,
Is dem mak' all dem big singer
Tan 'pon stage an have top ten single a sing.

Dough, sometimes I get a little tired
Of de all day hairdressers shop,
Where dem leave yuh under
De dreyer so long,
De chemical jus a bun of yuh head top,

I would stop have me head done,
An' let mi hair run free,
Put me hair in a cane row
Like mi used to wen' mi a pickney

But I have dis age old problem,
Dat I can't seem to shift,
Straignt'ning mek mi hair tuf
Like bamboo cane,
And all strany, strany and stiff,

So bring on de relaxer,
De straight'ning comb and tong,
Granny say it gone bad already,
But with yuh I can prove her wrong,

So, excuse mi if I'm a little under-whelmed
By yuh back to natural statement,
I'm neither political or spiritual,
I worship at de alter of
De fortnightly wash an' set,
Full conditioner steam treatment.

Blank

Chapter 3
Baby steps

Black acorns

Walk good
My Black Acorns,
I will plant you in the ground
with knowledge of your Black self,
Feed you with your true history,
Rain down my love and support,
So you can grow with dignity.

Walk good
My Black acorn
Stretch your branches to the skies
With your roots planted
In your history
You can grow with pride,

Paul Bogle died to give us freedom,
Martin Luther King died to give
Us a voice,
Malcolm X said 'by any means possible'
And I'm telling you that anything is
Possible in this life,

Black Acorns have the power
To stretch far and wide
So, walk good my Black Acorns,
Walk with pride

A call to arms

Why are you all laughing
And singing dat rap song
Pick up yuh weapons people
Don't you know there's war on.

Black boys without an education
Are dying on our streets,
Talk 'bout how 'im dis respeck him
Cho, yuh can't just turn yuh back a kiss yuh teet'

Children out dere having babies
Dress up in designer gear,
Everyone wants to be famous
Like it was fame dat brought us here.

Where once we were warriors
We anre now just Ethnic Minorities,
All races lumped together
So politicians can enforce
Racist asylum polices

No one knows how to fight back
Cas no one knows we're at war,
They gave us equal opportunity
The glass ceiling and
left crack cocaine at our door,

We say we are in control of our lives
We know who we be,
MTV has show us the video
That tells us this is our identity

And we fickle and brainwashed
Follow along like goat,
Big producer a mek big money
While we hold guns to each other throats.

Garvey, King and Malcolm X
Each turning in their graves
Dem tek we two steps forward
And bling bling and MTV cribs
Tun' we back into master and slave,

Every yout' on de street wants to be
A DJ or MC,
Play basketball, run 100 metre
Or play for Manchester FC

We tek we money an' buy
Name bran' like Moshino and Nike
Is like everyone else know say dem poor
And nobody never tell we

Can't you see that dis is a battlefield
Like D day or de Somme,
Can't you smell Black minds rotting?
Decaying without the African sun,

Pick up a book an' read each word
Is only knowledge can mek yuh grow,
We need to stretch back our han'
Grab back we history
Tell dem, dem wrong
No'ting no go so,

We are a mis-placed, displaced Diaspora
We are Africans split at de steams,
Is only since we were westernised
Suddenly we only have one dream

De dream to shake we tail end
On de little screen
Young girls in skirt so short
Me can almost see dem spleen,

We tink cas we win a few battles
Dat de fight over and' dun,
Tink say BNP a sleep
An' now dem a get ready fi come

So, why are you all laughing
And singing dat rap song
Pick up yuh book, yuh education yuh ambition
There is still work to be done

Moonlight

Who switched off de moon?
Put a blanket over de sun
Lef' Black mudders bawling
Cas we loose anudder son.

Who never polish de stars?
An' rolled up de big blue sky
A fardda stans wid shadows in 'is heart
As 'im watch 'im firs barn die.

Who forget to tell de sun
Dat it was dawn and it should rise
Eyes closed by murder
Only in justice can dey rise.

Who is up der painting de sky
Hate-we-one-anudder grey?
send we pickeny fe get education
Instead dem brains get wash wey

Who turn off de lights in our world?
Like a Black life doesn't matter
Each time de moon get switch off
Our lives like glass shatter

Who ever switch off de moon?
Has caused thousands of black tears to be shed
What a great dey it will be
When they stop killing Black pickney
Certifiably, irretrievably dead

Identity crisis
Nikisha mi dear yuh no hear de news
Say England get dem identity confused?
All dose years dem a talk 'bout we plus tree,
And how dem is all one great big family,
But now Scotland pick up him two something a garn,
Sey dem want devolution,
England hav' fe give back dem stone,
An ' if dem don't mine sharp
Dem soon have fe give back dem trone.

Nikisha me dear, what a shock,
When Scotland pick-up him grip
And start pack.
When referendum time
Scotland never joke,
From de outta Hebrides, come right dung
Everybody start vote,
But Nikisha me dear
Scotland never contented from time,
Dem have dem owner money,
Owner law, ever and dem owner crime,

Now is England plus two,
But when dem look in de corner;
Wales garn too,
Nikisha, how yuh mean yuh never hear,
Say Scotland and Wales broke out and garn clear,
Now is England plus one,

But over in Ireland dem a have a revolution,
Dem don't want independence
Dem want total exclusion,

Nikisha mi dear, what a ting,
Devolution send England identity into a spin.
Dem walk, walk in a everybody lan'
An' teef out dem tings an' say a fe dem,
Cars of dat everybody else know who dem be,
But now sake a devolution, England in a quandary

Nikisha, you must know how de story go,
How England walk wid him basket a pick, pick
People lan' a forture like dem a pick mango,
Dem tek de curry out a Indian
Tek way china dem tea,
And member sey dem did go a Africa
And tek wey you and me.

Nikisha, no fret 'bout dem and dem problem
Is about time dem understand
Dat de world was doing quite fine
without de Englishman

So Nikisha, next time yuh see a Englishman
A pat, pat himself front an' back
tell him, when him give back
We lan', we forture and we history,
We will give him, 'im identity back.

Little Twang

I wonder how many languages
Are spoken on dis lan'?
Everybody know 'bout English ,
French, Spanish and German,
There's Cantonese, Japanese
An' even outta Mongolian,
But I wonder if oonoo know 'bout
De one dem call little twang.

Me no mean de speaky-spokey
One dat oonoo use fi answer de phone,
Or de lar-de-dar voice dat yuh
Put on when smuddy come to call,
I don't mean 'O he'snot hare at
Thee moment can I take a massage?'
Voice garn up two octave,
Like you a whistle darg,
I'm taking your natural vocabulary
Dat yuh use when no one dey 'bout,
De 'give mi' de 'cooya' and 'kibber yuih mout',

Happl' , horang', hadvartizment,
Yuh a laugh at de pronunciation
But yuh all know what I'm talkin' 'bout
Dis is mudder tongue conversation,
Flim, cerfiticket, humbelance,
You a roll yuh eye an; snigger,
But dey were created out of adversity
By yuh owner ancestor,

Hard time de tek we,
Slave master cut out we tongue,
But we great, great grand-somebody
Tek old clothes and mek another one,

So, whedder yuh is Jamaican, Barbadian
Or from Trinidad,
Talk yuh talk, speak yuh speak
And when yuh do so hold up yuh head.
Black people tek bad something
and mek we owner slang,
Some people call it bad talking,
Me I call it a little twang.

Childhood

I remember the first time I discovered I could fly,
I would soar up above the rooftops,
Creating dreams out of air pie.

I remember a place in time,
When I could hold out my hand,
And make a chocolate covered palace for myself
From a tiny grain of sand.

I could climb mountains so high
That I could see God's shoes,
Touch clouds, rainbows and stars,
And say goodnight to the moon.

I remember the first time I saw the rain fall,
I thought the world was crying
And if no one made people laugh,
We would all be washed away
Into a giant human water fall.

Snow was a mystery to me,
When I first saw it on the ground,
Were the clouds to fat to stay up in the sky
And had to loose a few pounds.

Once apon a time I could smell
The colours of the rainbow,
I could hear the sun go
To the other side of the world

I remember a time when
My heat had wings,
I could take sadness and
Painful thoughts and turn
Them into dreams

My days were spun from gold,
My nights decorated with silver,
And in my head I had an army
Of red and yellow lollipops,
Armed with swords to protect me
From the night monster,

Once apon a time I could close my eyes
And dream and dream all day,
Of sugar coated,
Liquorice scented angels,
Who we never to tired to
Come out to play

Chapter 4
Man steps

Umbrella love

Without opening his mouth
His words fill my head,
His heart beats so fast
That it doesn't move at all
And you could mistakenly
Think he were dead.

His eyes have forgotten
How to shed tears
But the sound of him
Sobbing silently inside Is so loud
that I have to cover my ears.

When I stand really close to him
 Too close to him
I can hear the voices in his mind
They are paranoia and fear of rejection
They stand on either side,

He has learnt to keep his eyes open
So he can't see his own pain
Silently, he speaks volumes,
Through aggression
He has learnt to hide any shame,

He's as wide as an ocean
And stands mountain tall
But as I look into his face,
He has become foetus like and small

No one told me that men cry too,
That if you cut them they feel pain
No one warned me that without love to shield them
Men go rusty in the rain.

.The key to a man's heart

Kiss me ackee pod,
What a ting,
Mis Joseph fine a man
After all her long years of single ooman livin;.
It's been 15 years since mars Joseph lef',
Run off wid one a dem old time,
Air Jamaica cabin crew hostess.
She couldn't ardastan', why 'im l
Love fly un and dung,
An spen' out all dem likkle pension.
Not even bring back a cup of white rum fe she sip,
Till one day him just pack him grip,
Say him garn to de land of wood and water,
'pon a one way ticket.

Well dat was de end of man fe she,
Any man wey tink dem a pass thru,
Couldn't even get a cup a mint tea..

But, dat was den an dis is now,
And yuh see how ttngs turn out,
Every week she a mek a potatoe puddun,
Buy up all the ingredients and have dem put down,
De only word she would a say,
Is 'oh I'm making if for a friend'
Then 'pon valentines day,
She come in wid one ring,

De deacon from de Baptist church opposite Tesco,
Ask her to married him.
Hey, me mearly far-lay-tee,
When me see de big old sapphire and
Diamond cluster 'pon her lef' 'how a
Look back at me.
You see how life can be.
Mars joseph dye a Jamaica worse off dan you and me
De ooman tek wey every penny im de have,
 Now 'im under hot sun a fight darg fe piece a bread.
After all de pain an' shame,
Miss Joseph come get a good,
Good good, good man like mars Benjamin,
And all she had to do to secure him,
Was bake an' ole fashion Jamaican potato puddun

A warning to the Black man

Sometimes I sit and wonder,
Sometimes I feel so sad,
If our mothers and grandmothers
Coming to this country
Have turned all de black man mad,

If you look at de shape of those women
They were all big and broad,
Dem butty long out a back so
And dem chest garn abroad.

De Black man now, sey 'im no
Want no voluptuous women,
Say dem to much fe him,
Sey when 'im get more dan a handful
'im don't know what 'im doing,

'im warnt a ooman
Who butty flat like bammy
Who chest favour tow piece a toast,
With two ackee seed pon top if it.

Now if de man dem did have any sense at all
Dey would tek someone
Who have whole heap a carve an' crease,
Dat was de shape of our foremothers
And dem de strong like coconut tree.

Now tek my body for instance
Me have so many places to hide,
Yuh could lose your self for a week,
Just tink of all de fun we could have every night
Playing hide and seek,

No, man today say 'im want manga gal
You can use fi pick you teet'
Turn dem sideways in a one storm,
And breeze blow dem clear garn a Martinique.

Now I ain't here to cry dung slim gal,
We all have a right to be here,
But I tink de way oonoo man is
Carrying on is damn disgusting,
And I don't tink is fair,

But if you want to ride stick insect
 When big sexy women is here
 You can tek de two grape wey dem have
And I will keep wey me have over here,

But Black man I giving you a warning,
I only hope you can hear,
Appreciate de big butty big chested Black women
Is cos of she, why you is here.

Tears

Last night as you came to me,
I cried.

As your love flowed into me,
My love flowed out of me,
I cried.

As your body came to meet me,
My nipples stood up to greet you,
The feminine between my legs,
Licked her lips, stretched out herself,
And welcomed you,
But inside I cried.

As I sucked apon your sweetness,
Run my tongue over your stiffness,
Took all of you, whole into me,
Inside I cried.

As you tasted the cherry at my centre,
Gently sucking at it's seed,
Inside I cried.

In to me, out of me,
As you interrogated the inner me,
With the outer muscle that is you,
Stretching my mind beyond the limits of the G spot,
I cried.

Your love flowed into me,
My love flowed out of me,
But the ring on your finger,
Tells me that your love is a lie,
So I cried and cried

Black Sunshine

I woke up with Black sunshine in my bed
It was sleek and muscular,
Like playing hide and seek
With the moon each night had kept it toned

Sunshine lay between cotton sheets
Open, care free,
Judging no-one
Labelling no –one,
Not even me.

Sunshine took a handful
Of night-time, wrapped it gently,
Oh so gently around me
Then held me by my mind
And we danced,

,

I watched sunshine,
My Black sunshine
Breath in invisible thoughts,
Breath out achievable dreams

Like Lego bricks
We fit together,
Click together,
And on and on we danced

I kissed my sunshine
My black sunshine
Who rose up to meet me
All else forgotten,
And it was the start
Of a new day.

Clearing out my heart

I've held you in my heart for too long
You're taking up too much room,
The space you hold in my left ventricle
Next to my favourite colour,
My most played love song,
My first kiss,
This space needs to be vacated.

You are my old broom
You know me well,
But new broom still sweep clean,
So please leave the building
You are causing an obstruction

Deaf Girls
Are you listening?
He said he was too tired to make love

    Are you listening?

He said he was going out with his breddrin,
Doesn't know what time, what day, what year
He will come back

    Are you listening

He's got better things to do than be with you,
You are last on he's 'to do list' last on his mind

    Are you listening

Is his mobile phone broken, it always cuts off when you call him

He doesn't want to talk about 'it'
There's nothing to say, just leave a message on his voicemail, for the hundredth time.
So he can ignore it, ignore you

Meaning you bore him

    Are you listening

Can't take you out on valentines Day, or any day, for
that meal he promised. The game's on the T.V.

Are you Listening

Then you argue, tell him 'bout himself,

Yes that is the door you can hear slamming on your re-
lationship,
His body just left.
But his mind, his attention, his attentiveness, his sharing
his caring, his smile, his help, his support, his concern
for your wellbeing, his soft touch, his gentle moan as
you made love, his attempts to make you simile, his en-
quiring about your day, his love ,they were already gone

Are you listening?

You are standing there with your moth open
Tears in your eyes,
Saying you don't understand.
When did it go wrong,
Why didn't he tell you how he was feeling?
Why didn't he tell you he didn't love you
That you bored him,

He did, you just weren't listening

Blank

A tree without roots,
Is just a stick